We Worship and Pray
The Mass & Traditional Catholic Prayers
Reproducible Handouts for Intermediate Grades

Francine M. O'Connor

Active Learning for Catholic Kids
Hi-Time✷Pflaum
Dayton, OH

We Worship and Pray
The Mass & Traditional Catholic Prayers
Reproducible Handouts for Intermediate Grades
Active Learning for Catholic Kids
Francine M. O'Connor

Cover design by Larissa Qvick
Interior design by Patricia Lynch

The Scripture quotations contained herein are from the *New Revised Standard Version of the Bible:* Catholic Edition, ©1993 and 1989 by the Division of Christian Education of the National Council of the Churches of Christ in the U.S.A. All rights reserved. Used by permission.

©2000 Hi-Time✳Pflaum, Dayton, OH 45449. All rights reserved. Photocopying of the material herein is permitted by the publisher for noncommercial use. The permission line must appear on each reproduced page. Any other type of reproduction, transmittal, storage, or retrieval, in any form or by any means, whether electronic or mechanical, including recording, is not permitted without the written consent of the publisher.

ISBN: 0-937997-55-2

Contents

The Mass

Greeting	We Gather As Family
Penitential Rite	We Confess Our Sins
Liturgy of the Word	God Speaks, We Listen
Profession of Faith: Part 1	Creed Crossword
Profession of Faith: Part 2	In My Own Words
Prayers of the Faithful: Part 1	We Pray for One Another
Prayers of the Faithful: Part 2	Christian Love
The Offertory	We Give Our Gifts
Liturgy of the Eucharist	Praise and Thanksgiving
The Lord's Prayer	Praying as Jesus Prayed
The Sign of Peace	We Offer the Peace of Christ
Communion	We Receive Jesus
Blessing and Dismissal	Go in Peace

Prayers and Prayer Forms

Rosary	Praying the Rosary (4 pages)
Scripture	Praying with the Bible
Intercession of Saints	Saints Can Help Us Pray
Devotions	Nine Times Better
Pilgrimages	Prayer Places
The Divine Office: Part 1	Turning Hours into Prayers
The Divine Office: Part 2	Prayer-Time Clock
Stations of the Cross	The Road to Glory (2 pages)

Notes to Teacher .... (See Inside Back Cover)

We Gather As Family

Name _____

Whenever we go to Mass, it is like a giant family reunion. We gather with our whole parish family. We express our joy in being together, and we sing or say a prayer of praise to God. In churches all over the world, other members of God's family are gathering to pray along with us.

Solve this acrostic to learn what God told us about praying together. First, answer the clues, then transfer the letters to the corresponding numbers below.

Horn sound ___ ___ ___ ___
            11 8   9 11

A jewel for your finger ___ ___ ___ ___
                        24 35 28 19

Common grain used in bread ___ ___ ___ ___ ___
                            1 22 40 36   6

Trick or ___ ___ ___ ___ ___
         21 13 25 16 48

Sleepy, exhausted ___ ___ ___ ___ ___
                  38 27 10 34 26

Bambi, for one ___ ___ ___ ___
               26   3 14 17

Twelve months ___ ___ ___ ___
              30 23 20   4

One who digs coal for a living ___ ___ ___ ___ ___
                               37 27 31   5 41

Strong breeze ___ ___ ___ ___
               7 27 46 26

Opposite of low ___ ___ ___ ___
                39 27 47   2

Where your brain is located ___ ___ ___ ___
                            12 15 32 26

Toddler's name for mother ___ ___ ___ ___ ___
                          33 45 44 29 30

A favorite Easter meat ___ ___ ___
                       49 43 51

Scouts do a good one every day ___ ___ ___ ___
                               26 42 50 26

Three minus two ___ ___ ___
                 9 28 18

" ___ ___ ___ ___ ___ ___ ___ ___ ___ ___ ___ ___ ___ ___ ___ ___ ___ ___
   1   2   3   4   5   6   7   8   9 10 11 12 13 14 15 16 17 18

___ ___ ___ ___ ___ ___ ___ ___ ___ ___ ___ ___ ___ ___ ___ ___,
19 20 21 22 23 24 25 26 27 28 29 30 31 32 33 34

___ ___ ___ ___ ___ ___ ___ ___ ___ ___ ___ ___ ___ ___ ___ ___ ___."
35 36 37 38 39 40 41 42 43 44 45 46 47 48 49 50 51

(Matthew 18:20)

©2000 Hi-Time•Pflaum, Dayton, OH 45449 (800-543-4383). Permission is granted by the publisher to reproduce this page for classroom use only.

We Confess Our Sins

Name _____

During Mass, after we greet our church family, we remember those not-too-loving things we have done. We ask God and our brothers and sisters to forgive us. How many unloving acts can you find and circle in the hidden square?

Word List

First, we remember times when we have been...

DISHONEST   LAZY
DISOBEDIENT   MEAN
GRUMPY   PRIDEFUL
JEALOUS   SELFISH
UNCARING   UNFAIR

Then we tell God we are sorry for times when we...

FORGET TO PRAY

```
D A E P R I D E F U L I L F C
I M Q V U Y I B G I D Z U R N
S K O S N W S A D F B X T P L
O I M Q C U H V L A Z Y R N J
B W J C A F O U N F A I R D X
E Q E L R O N D G R U M P Y I
D H A U I Y E C P G D E Z V R
I H L J N M S O R F S A N K I
E W O Z G A T E K M G N H B X
N O U C I T L O S Q T P N J D
T J S S E L F I S H P R Y V O
J M S G W A E L Q F B X T N K
G K R O S Y A E G B Z T P L H
E O H M Q U Y C E Z V R N J F
F D G J O S W A C X T P K H B
```

©2000 Hi-Time•Pflaum, Dayton, OH 45449 (800-543-4383). Permission is granted by the publisher to reproduce this page for classroom use only.

God Speaks, We Listen

Name _____

During the Liturgy of the Word at Mass, we listen to three readings from the Bible. In the first reading, we hear stories of God and the people from the Old Testament. Next we listen to special letters from the leaders of the early church. Before the third reading, called the Gospel, we stand and sing "Alleluia." The Gospel contains the words of Jesus himself, stories he told to teach us about God's love.

1. Briefly describe a story you remember from the Bible.

   _____
   _____
   _____
   _____

2. What does this story mean to you?

   _____
   _____
   _____

3. From which part of the Bible does this story come?

   ☐ Old Testament   ☐ Letters   ☐ Gospel

4. If you were the preacher at Mass, how would you explain God's message in this story to everyone?

   _____
   _____
   _____
   _____

(Use the back of this paper if you need more room for your answers.)

©2000 Hi-Time•Pflaum, Dayton, OH 45449 (800-543-4383). Permission is granted by the publisher to reproduce this page for classroom use only.

Creed Crossword

Name _____

During every Mass, we pray the Profession of Faith—the Nicene Creed—which is a summary of what we believe as Catholics. The answers to this crossword will be familiar words from the Creed.

Across

2 The first person of the Trinity, God the _____
5 The body of people with whom we share our faith
6 Divinely inspired writers of the Old Testament who wrote about their times and the future.
8 Where we all live
11 The Roman ruler of Judea at the time of the crucifixion (2 words)
13 The son of God
15 The mother of God and of us all (2 words)
16 A place of eternal happiness
17 Having unlimited power

Down

1 What the Creator gave us
3 The event we celebrate on Easter
4 Third person of the Trinity (2 words)
7 The first sacrament we receive
9 Having succession of authority from the twelve chosen disciples
10 Whole; entire
12 What we seek when we are sorry for doing wrong
14 Universal
18 Spiritual; close to God

©2000 Hi-Time∗Pflaum, Dayton, OH 45449 (800-543-4383). Permission is granted by the publisher to reproduce this page for classroom use only.

In My Own Words

Name _____

Reflect on the Creed as you have learned to say it at Mass, then write in your own words why you believe each of the following statements.

I believe in God, the Father.

_____
_____
_____
_____

I believe in Jesus, God's son.

_____
_____
_____
_____

I believe in the Holy Spirit.

_____
_____
_____
_____

I believe in the Catholic Church.

_____
_____
_____
_____

©2000 Hi-Time✶Pflaum, Dayton, OH 45449 (800-543-4383). Permission is granted by the publisher to reproduce this page for classroom use only.

We Pray for One Another

Name _____

When families gather, they often discuss things that worry them and things that make them happy. With our church family, we also share our joys and our problems. During Mass, at the Prayers of the Faithful, we pray for one another, for all members of the church, for people in our communities, and for our nation. As Christians, we care about others as Jesus cares about all of us.

There are many ways of showing love. This is a rebus story about love. After reading the rebus story, solve the puzzle on the second page.

God's love shows through all creation: 🌳, 🌷, ☀️, 🌙, ⭐⭐, and even our 🐱🐶.

God's greatest love gift was 🧍 (Jesus).

Jesus showed his love by being born in a 🏠 (stable),

by sending the 🕊️ to live in each ♥️,

by coming to us in the 🍷 (chalice), and by dying for us on the ✝️.

We show our love together with all of God's 👨‍👩‍👶 (family),

whenever we pray together in ⛪.

©2000 HI-Time※Pflaum, Dayton, OH 45449 (800-543-4383). Permission is granted by the publisher to reproduce this page for classroom use only.

Christian Love

Name _____

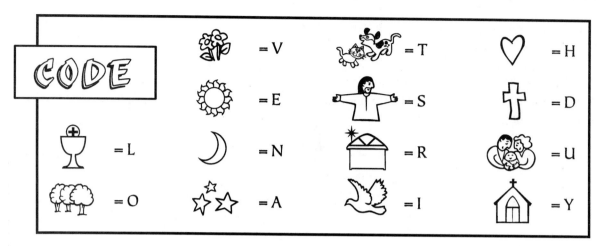

Use the Code above to solve this puzzle.
When you have decoded the message, you will discover Jesus' command about love.

" L O V E

   O N E

   A N O T H E R

   A S

   I

   H A V E

   L O V E D

   Y O U ." (John 15:12)

We Give Our Gifts

Name _____

During the Offertory of the Mass, we bring our gifts to God and ask God's blessing on them. We bring the bread and wine for communion, and sometimes we bring other examples of good things God has given us. But what gift does God most want from us? Solve this acrostic puzzle to find out.

1. A thick woodland

__ __ __ __ __ __
14 24 8 20 22 4

2. You talk with it and eat with it.

__ __ __ __ __
31 17 11 18 2

3. A ripple on the ocean's surface

__ __ __ __
1 3 6 32

4. A boat that carries cars across a river

__ __ __ __ __
28 5 16 30 9

5. Covered with a thin layer of dirt

__ __ __ __ __
12 25 22 4 23

6. An image cast by sunlight

__ __ __ __ __ __
22 19 3 26 29 1

7. Creme-filled chocolate cookie

__ __ __ __
13 21 7 27

8. A round toy with a string

__ __ __ __
9 15 23 10

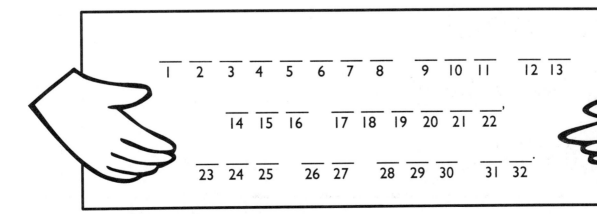

__ __ __ __ __ __ __ __ __ __ __ __ __
1 2 3 4 5 6 7 8 9 10 11 12 13

__ __ __ __ __ __ __ __ __,
14 15 16 17 18 19 20 21 22

__ __ __ __ __ __ __ __ __ __.
23 24 25 26 27 28 29 30 31 32

©2000 Hi-Time*Pflaum, Dayton, OH 45449 (800-543-4383). Permission is granted by the publisher to reproduce this page for classroom use only.

Praise and Thanksgiving

Name _____

How do you give a gift to someone you love? First you choose your gift with care, recalling all the person has done for you. Then you add a personal card or note to thank the person for all he or she has done for you. Finally, you wrap your gift in festive paper to show that it is something special.

During Mass, there is a particular time when we prepare to give and receive gifts of love.

We Remember the One We Love

We remember the wondrous love of Jesus as we offer our gifts at the altar.

Holy, holy, holy, Lord, God of power and might, heaven and earth are full of your glory. Hosanna in the highest. Blessed is he who comes in the name of the Lord. Hosanna in the highest.

Our Personal Note of Faith

We listen to Jesus' words at the Last Supper and add a note of faith in him and his promises.

*Christ has died, Christ is risen,
Christ will come again.*

Wrapped in Jesus' Love

We wrap our gift in Jesus' great love and prepare to receive his Body and Blood.

Through him, with him, and in him, in the unity of the Holy Spirit, all glory and honor is yours, almighty Father, for ever and ever. Amen.

Can you name the prayer at Mass into which all of these prayers are "wrapped"? Solve this acrostic and you will have it!

1. A place to sit down

   __ __ __ __ __
   11 4 14 7 17

2. A beam of sunlight

   __ __ __
   6 5 15

3. The celebrant at Mass

   __ __ __ __ __ __
   12 6 10 16 8 9

4. A beating organ that gives you life

   __ __ __ __ __
   4 1 14 6 9

5. Smash, flatten

   __ __ __ __ __
   3 13 2 8 4

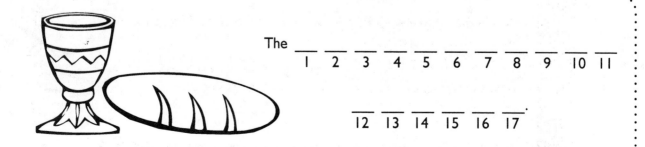

The __ __ __ __ __ __ __ __ __ __ __
    1 2 3 4 5 6 7 8 9 10 11

__ __ __ __ __ __ .
12 13 14 15 16 17

Praying as Jesus Prayed

Name _____

Often, when Jesus prayed, he would go off by himself to a quiet place and talk to his Father. When the disciples asked him to teach them how to pray, he taught them a prayer that is now the best known prayer among all Christians—the Our Father, or the Lord's Prayer. We pray it together at each Mass before we receive Communion. You can also use Jesus' prayer as an example for a prayer of your own, to pray during your own quiet time with God.

Fill in the blanks with the correct words to finish Jesus' prayer, then circle those same words in the Quiet-Time Prayer. See how our own prayers can imitate Jesus' prayer.

Our __ __ __ __ __ __, who art in __ __ __ __ __ __,

hallowed be thy __ __ __ __.

Thy kingdom come, thy will be done, on earth as it is in heaven.

Give us this day, our daily __ __ __ __ __,

and __ __ __ __ __ __ __ us our trespasses

as we forgive those who trespass against us.

And lead us not into __ __ __ __ __ __ __ __ __ __,

but deliver us from __ __ __ __.

Amen

Quiet-Time Prayer

Lord Jesus,

When you prayed you always called on your Father in heaven. Just to say God's name is my prayer.

I praise God for giving me everything I need to live in this world—the air I breath, the bread I eat, and the water that quenches my thirst.

I know that God always forgives my sins. I promise to forgive those people who make me angry.

Lord, help me to avoid the temptation to do wrong. Protect my mind from evil thoughts and lead my heart to all things good.

Amen

We Offer the Peace of Christ

Name _____

At Mass, before we receive the Body and Blood of Jesus, we turn to our neighbor and say "Peace be with you." This is what Jesus told his disciples before he returned to heaven. Complete the crossword below to identify some symbols of Christ's peace.

Across

1. One sent by Jesus to guide and teach us (two words)
3. Common name for when we receive the Body and Blood of Christ
5. Sacrament given to us at the Last Supper
8. Three Persons in one God
10. Our Savior

Down

2. When Jesus rose from the tomb
4. One who reads God's Word at Mass
6. The Word of God as written in the Bible
7. The way we talk with God
9. A time of worship with our church family

©2000 Hi-Time*Pflaum, Dayton, OH 45449 (800-543-4383). Permission is granted by the publisher to reproduce this page for classroom use only.

We Receive Jesus

Name _____

Together we go to the altar of God and receive the body and blood of Jesus. When we eat the bread and drink the wine, we are one with Jesus and with one another.

Using the code below, solve the puzzle to find the promise Jesus makes us about the Eucharist.

(John 6:51)

Code

A = I	G = B	M = N
B = A	H = R	N = F
C = M	I = D	O = V
D = T	J = C	P = S
E = H	K = O	Q = L
F = E	L = W	R = G

Go in Peace

Name _____

When Mass is over, the priest or deacon tells us, "Go in peace to love and serve the Lord." We have received the special gift of Jesus in our hearts. Now, like Jesus, we can go and serve others with love.

A Mobile of Service

Make a class mobile of service. Using carbon paper, transfer the dove pattern to posterboard and cut out your dove. Write your name on one side of the dove with a bright marker or crayon. On the other side of the dove, write some way that you can serve God or others. Punch out the hole in your dove, thread a piece of yarn through the hole, and hang your dove with the others on the mobile.

©2000 HI-TIME✴Pflaum, Dayton, OH 45449 (800-543-4383). Permission is granted by the publisher to reproduce this page for classroom use only.

THE MYSTERIES OF THE ROSARY

JOYFUL MYSTERIES
(Monday, Thursday, Sundays of Advent)

1. The Annunciation
2. The Visitation
3. The Nativity
4. The Presentation
5. The Finding in the Temple

SORROWFUL MYSTERIES
(Tuesday, Friday, Sundays of Lent)

1. The Agony in the Garden
2. The Scourging
3. The Crowning with Thorns
4. The Way of the Cross
5. The Crucifixion

GLORIOUS MYSTERIES
(Wednesday, Saturday, remaining Sundays of year)

1. The Resurrection
2. The Ascension of Jesus
3. The Descent of the Holy Spirit
4. The Assumption of Mary
5. Mary's Coronation

©2000 Hi-Time✤Pflaum, Dayton, OH 45449 (800-543-4383). Permission is granted by the publisher to reproduce this page for classroom use only.

HOW TO SAY THE ROSARY

1. Make the sign of the cross.
2. Pray the Apostles' Creed on the crucifix.
3. Pray the Lord's Prayer on the large bead.
4. Pray the Hail Mary on the three small beads.
5. On the next large bead, pray the Glory Be to the Father, call to mind the first mystery, and pray the Lord's Prayer.
6. Pray a Hail Mary on each of the next ten beads.
7. On the next large bead, pray the Glory Be, call to mind the second mystery. Pray the Lord's Prayer, and begin the second decade of Hail Marys.
8. Continue this pattern of prayers until you have finished all five decades.

Note: Many people like to add the Prayer of Fatima after each decade, and the Hail, Holy Queen prayer at the end of the rosary.

Labels on diagram: GLORY BE, OUR FATHER, HAIL MARYS, GLORY BE, OUR FATHER, HAIL MARYS, OUR FATHER, APOSTLES' CREED

Marian Feasts

Throughout the year, we celebrate special days that are related to Mary's life or to our belief in Mary. To make a record of these days for yourself, match the right feast with its description. Write the name of the feast in the space provided.

January 1: This title sums up the Church's belief in Mary and the important role she plays in the history of Christianity.
_____

March 25: The angel Gabriel told Mary she was to be the mother of the Messiah.
_____

May 31: After learning she was to have a baby, Mary went to see her cousin Elizabeth, who was also expecting a child.
_____

August 15: Mary died and was taken into heaven.
_____

December 8: Throughout her life, Mary was without sin. She identified herself with this title when she appeared to St. Bernadette in Lourdes, France, in 1858.
_____

December 12: On this day in 1531, near Mexico City, Mary appeared as an Aztec maiden to Juan Diego. A beautiful cathedral was built and named in her honor on the spot she appeared.
_____

- The Assumption
- The Annunciation
- Our Lady of Guadalupe
- The Visitation
- Immaculate Conception
- Mary, Mother of God

©2000 Hi-Time*Pflaum, Dayton, OH 45449 (800-543-4383). Permission is granted by the publisher to reproduce this page for classroom use only.

THE APOSTLES' CREED

I believe in God, the Father almighty,
creator of heaven and earth.

I believe in Jesus Christ, God's only Son, our Lord.
He was conceived by the power of the Holy Spirit,
born of the Virgin Mary,
suffered under Pontius Pilate,
was crucified, died, and was buried.

He descended to the dead.

On the third day, he rose again.

He ascended into heaven
and is seated at the right hand of the Father.

He will come again to judge
the living and the dead.

I believe in the Holy Spirit,
the holy catholic Church,
the communion of saints,
the forgiveness of sins,
the resurrection of the body,
and live everlasting.

Amen

HAIL, HOLY QUEEN

Hail, holy Queen, mother of mercy,
our life, our sweetness, and our hope!

To thee do we cry, poor banished children of Eve;
to thee do we send up our sighs,
mourning and weeping in this valley of tears.

Turn, then, most gracious advocate,
thine eyes of mercy toward us;
and after this, our exile,
show unto us the blessed fruit
of thy womb, Jesus.

O clement, O loving, O sweet Virgin Mary!

©2000 HI-Time❊Pflaum, Dayton, OH 45449 (800-543-4383). Permission is granted by the publisher to reproduce this page for classroom use only.

GLORY BE TO THE FATHER

Glory be to the Father,
and to the Son,
and to the Holy Spirit.
As it was in the beginning, is now,
and ever shall be,
world without end.

Amen

THE LORD'S PRAYER
"Our Father"

Our Father, who art in heaven,
hallowed be thy name.
Thy kingdom come; thy will be done
on earth as it is in heaven.
Give us this day our daily bread,
and forgive us our trespasses
as we forgive those who trespass against us;
and lead us not into temptation,
but deliver us from evil.

Amen

THE HAIL MARY

Hail Mary, full of grace;
the Lord is with thee.
Blessed art thou among women
and blessed is the fruit of thy womb, Jesus.
Holy Mary, Mother of God,
pray for us sinners,
now and at the hour of our death.

Amen

THE PRAYER OF FATIMA

O my Jesus, forgive us our sins.
Save us from the fires of hell,
lead all souls to heaven,
especially those who have most need
of your mercy.

Amen

©2000 Hi-Time✶Pflaum, Dayton, OH 45449 (800-543-4383). Permission is granted by the publisher to reproduce this page for classroom use only.

Praying with the Bible

Name _____

Jesus knew every story ever written about God and God's people. Often, when he prayed, he prayed with these Bible stories. You can do this too. Use the code to solve the cryptogram and discover a Scripture prayer of thanksgiving and praise.

"I WILL GIVE THANKS TO THE LORD WITH MY WHOLE HEART; I WILL TELL OF ALL YOUR WONDERFUL DEEDS. I WILL BE GLAD AND EXULT IN YOU; I WILL SING PRAISE TO YOUR NAME." (Psalm 9:1-2)

Code

A = I	J = H	R = M
B = W	K = A	S = Y
C = L	L = N	T = F
D = G	M = K	V = U
E = V	N = S	W = B
H = E	O = R	Y = X
I = T	P = O	X = P
	Q = D	

Saints Can Help Us Pray

Name _____

We can call on the saints to pray with us and they will add their prayers to ours. All we have to do is ask them. Some saints are patrons of special favors, others have a wonderful understanding of our problems. See if you can match the saints on the left with their special areas of help on the right.

___ 1. Saint Francis   a. Mother to Jesus and to all God's children

___ 2. Saint Anthony   b. Patron saint of Ireland

___ 3. Saint Jude   c. Patron saint of lost youth

___ 4. Saint Thérèse of Lisieux   d. Stepfather to Jesus and patron of all fathers

___ 5. Saint Joseph   e. Patron saint of animals and pets

___ 6. Saint John Bosco   f. Patroness of missions

___ 7. Blessed Virgin Mary   g. Patron saint of impossible cases

___ 8. Saint Patrick   h. Patron saint of lost articles

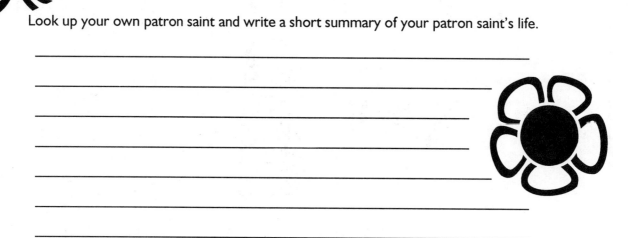

Look up your own patron saint and write a short summary of your patron saint's life.

_____
_____
_____
_____
_____

How can you follow your patron saint's example in your own life?

_____
_____
_____

©2000 Hi-Time•Pflaum, Dayton, OH 45449 (800-543-4383). Permission is granted by the publisher to reproduce this page for classroom use only.

Nine Times Better

Name _____

The Church has a tradition of repeating prayers in groups of nine—nine hours, nine days, nine weeks, or nine months. Each year, many churches hold a nine-day or nine-week prayer gathering to Our Lady of Perpetual Help, Our Lady of Guadalupe, Saint Jude, Saint Anthony, or the special patrons of their parishes. Solve the rebus to find out what we call this tradition of prayer-times-nine.

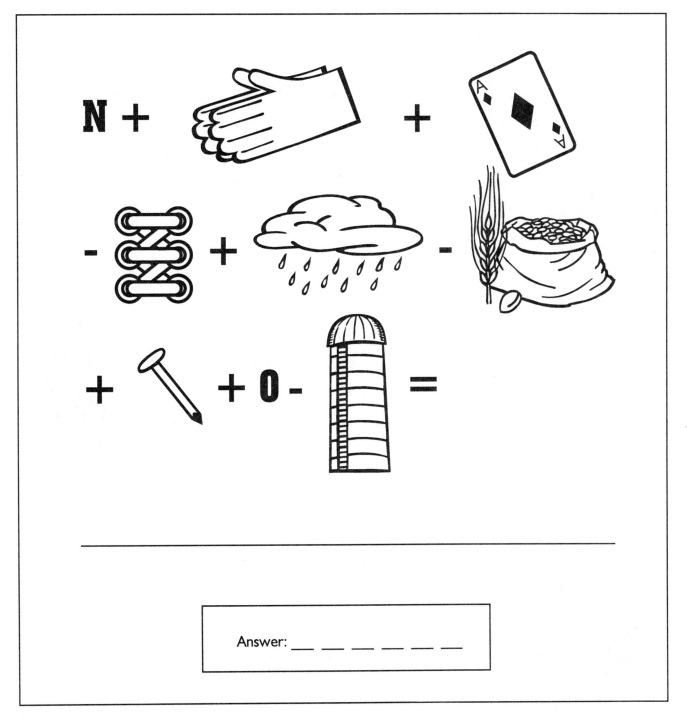

Answer: __ __ __ __ __

©2000 HI-TIME*Pflaum, Dayton, OH 45449 (800-543-4383). Permission is granted by the publisher to reproduce this page for classroom use only.

Prayer Places

Name _____

Many people travel great distances to go to a particular shrine. Such a journey is called a pilgrimage. A shrine is a special place dedicated to the prayer-power of a certain saint. Some shrines mark sites where our Lady has appeared or a miracle has occurred. Can you match the following shrines with their stories?

DPAALGUEU

Juan Diego was a simple Aztec Indian peasant. One day, he met a beautiful lady who told him she wanted a church built on the hill where she stood. The Lady performed the miracle of the roses so the bishop would believe Juan Diego.

The shrine is named after Our Lady of

_____.

SDLREOU

Saint Bernadette Soubirous was only a child when Our Lady appeared to her. The lady told Bernadette to wash in the stream near a grotto. Today, people travel to the miraculous waters seeking cures from their illnesses.

The shrine is dedicated to Our Lady of

_____.

TIAAMF

Three children were gathering wood for their parents. Suddenly, one of the children fell to her knees. She had seen a vision of Our Lady in a tree. Regularly after that, Our Lady appeared to the children with a message for the people. People followed the children to the place where Our Lady appeared. They would kneel and pray the Rosary with the children, but only the children could see Our Lady.

This shrine is dedicated to Our Lady of

_____.

©2000 Hi-Time❖Pflaum, Dayton, OH 45449 (800-543-4383). Permission is granted by the publisher to reproduce this page for classroom use only.

Turning Hours into Prayers

Name _____

Priests, brothers, sisters, and many lay people all over the world pray a series of prayers every day and every night at designated hours. These prayers are from Scripture and other sources. Monks and other groups of people who live in a community most often pray these prayers together—often singing or chanting them; others pray them alone. But everyone prays them at the same hour of each day.

One name for this prayer form is The Divine Office, but another is hidden in the code-word below.

First, cut out the clock face and hour hand of the Prayer-Time Clock. Paste the clock face onto a piece of posterboard or cardboard. Punch a small hole in the center of the clock and another in the base of the hour hand. Attach the hour hand with a paper fastener that allows the hand to move.

Referring to the puzzle, place the hour hand on the time indicated by each clue. Write that letter on the first blank. Continue until you have solved the puzzle and discovered the name of this special prayer form.

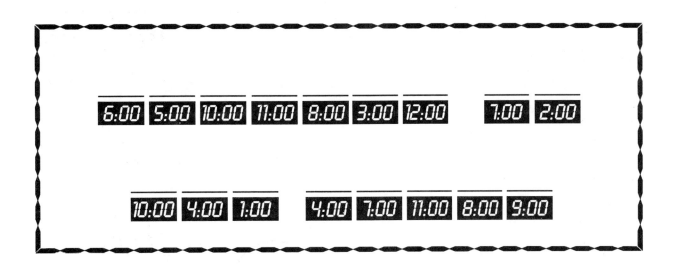

Now solve this message to find out something else about this special way to pray.

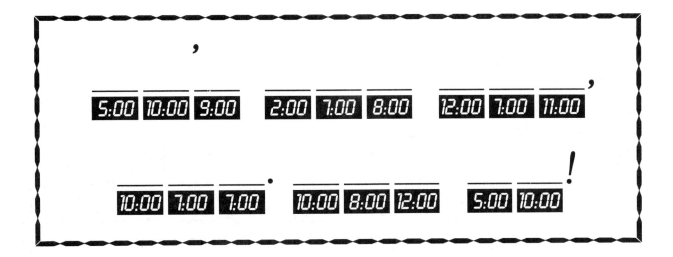

©2000 Hi-Time*Pflaum, Dayton, OH 45449 (800-543-4383). Permission is granted by the publisher to reproduce this page for classroom use only.

Prayer-Time Clock

Name _____

©2000 Hi-Time•Pflaum, Dayton, OH 45449 (800-543-4383). Permission is granted by the publisher to reproduce this page for classroom use only.

The Road to Glory

When we pray the Stations of the Cross, we relive Jesus' long, slow journey to Calvary. As we walk with Jesus, we remember his great love and we pray to walk in that love always.

Name _____

First Station
Jesus is condemned to die.

Jesus was condemned for something he did not do. Have you ever been accused or punished for something you did not do? How did you feel?

_____
_____

Jesus, at times life seems so unfair. In your name, I will try to speak out when I see injustice and to defend those who are treated unfairly. Amen.

Second Station
Jesus takes up his cross.

A long way to go, a heavy cross to carry. Name your own cross—illness, family problems, difficulties at school. What or who helps you carry your cross?

_____
_____

Dearest Lord, give me strength to carry my cross each day. Amen.

Third Station
Jesus falls for the first time.

Weakened by his beating, Jesus falls to his knees. Even in following Jesus, we sometimes slip and fall. When you fail to follow Jesus, what do you do to get back on the right track?

_____
_____

Dear Jesus, help me to begin anew every time I turn away from you. Amen.

Fourth Station
Jesus meets his mother.

Mary's heart is broken by the pain of her son. List something that makes your mother or father happy. Can you help make this happen?

_____
_____

Dearest Jesus, show me the way to love my parents as you loved Mary and Joseph. Amen.

Fifth Station
Simon helps Jesus carry his cross.

The soldiers force Simon of Cyrene to help Jesus carry his cross. How can you help someone who is carrying a heavy cross?

_____
_____

Jesus, teach me to help you by helping others. Amen.

Sixth Station
Veronica wipes the face of Jesus.

Veronica reaches out to wipe away the signs of suffering in Jesus' face. Name two ways you can bring a smile to someone's face.

_____
_____

Jesus, there is so much sadness in this world. Please help me to bring happiness and peace to others. Amen.

Seventh Station
Jesus falls for the second time.

Jesus is exhausted. The journey is so long, the cross so heavy. Think about a time when you felt so tired you just wanted to quit. What did you do about it?

_____
_____

Dear Jesus, give me the strength to keep trying, even when things get rough. Amen.

©2000 Hi-Time✴Pflaum, Dayton, OH 45449 (800-543-4383). Permission is granted by the publisher to reproduce this page for classroom use only.

Eighth Station
Jesus meets the crying women.

Jesus tells the women not to cry for him, but for all God's suffering children. Name one example of suffering in the world and one thing you can do to help the situation.

_____
_____

Lord, help me to wipe away the tears of those who suffer. Amen.

Ninth Station
Jesus falls for the third time.

Jesus' journey is almost over when he falls again. What would you like to say to Jesus at this time?

_____
_____

Dear Jesus, I realize how much I need your help. Thank you for not giving up on me. Amen.

Tenth Station
Soldiers strip Jesus of his clothing.

The soldiers took away Jesus' robes but they could not take away his dignity and ultimate glory. Reflect on a time that you felt embarrassed or humiliated. How did you handle it?

_____
_____

Dearest Jesus, help me to keep my priorities straight and to remember that God is with me even during hard times. Amen.

Eleventh Station
Jesus is nailed to the cross.

The soldiers hammer the nails into Jesus' hands and feet. List one way you can serve as Jesus' hands and one way you can serve as his feet.

_____
_____

Dear Jesus, please lead me in your way of love so that I can learn to be your hands and feet in this world. Amen.

Twelfth Station
Jesus dies on the cross.

After three hours of suffering, Jesus dies on the cross and someone cries out, "Clearly, this was the Son of God." What do you find hard to believe? What helps you find the truth?

_____
_____

Lord, grant me faith, especially during the darkest moments in my life. Amen.

Thirteenth Station
Jesus is taken down from the cross.

Mary waits below the cross to take her son into her arms. It is a very sad time for her. When you are sad, what or who do you find most comforts you?

_____
_____

Mary, you had much sadness in your life, yet you never stopped doing God's will. Help me to be brave and faithful when I face difficulties in my life. Amen.

Fourteenth Station
Jesus is buried in the tomb.

This looks like the end of a very sad story, but it is really just the beginning. Explain why.

_____
_____

Dear God, thank you for sending your son to show us the way to live—even if life gets very hard. Thank you for your promise to us of our "happy ending." Amen.

Concluding Prayer

Dear God, this journey has been long and sad. But we know that soon we will celebrate Jesus' victory over death and his glory as your son. Help me to walk his footsteps with faith, courage, love, and determination. I ask this in his name. Amen.